A FIRST LOOK AT DUCKS, GEESE, AND SWANS

By Millicent E. Selsam and Joyce Hunt

Illustrated by Harriett Springer

WALKER AND COMPANY  NEW YORK

First published in the United States of America in 1990
by Walker Publishing Company, Inc.

Published simultaneously in Canada by Thomas Allen & Son
Canada, Limited, Markham, Ontario

Library of Congress Cataloging-in-Publication Data

Selsam, Millicent Ellis.
A first look at ducks, geese, and swans / by Millicent E. Selsam
and Joyce Hunt : illustrated by Harriett Springer.
Summary: Examines the differences and similarities of ducks,
geese, and swans.
ISBN 0-8027-6975-6.—ISBN 0-8027-6976-4 (reinf.)
1. Ducks—Juvenile literature. 2. Geese—Juvenile literature.
3. Swans—Juvenile literature. [1. Ducks. 2. Geese. 3. Swans.]
I. Hunt, Joyce. II. Springer, Harriett, ill. III. Title.
QL696.A52S44   1990
598.4′1—dc20   90-12697

Printed in the United States of America

2 4 6 8 10 9 7 5 3 1

A FIRST LOOK AT SERIES

LEAVES
FISH
MAMMALS
BIRDS
INSECTS
FROGS AND TOADS
SNAKE, LIZARDS, AND OTHER REPTILES
ANIMALS WITH BACKBONES
ANIMALS WITHOUT BACKBONES
FLOWERS
THE WORLD OF PLANTS
MONKEYS AND APES
SHARKS
WHALES
CATS
DOGS
HORSES
SEASHELLS
DINOSAURS
SPIDERS
ROCKS
BIRD NESTS
KANGAROOS, KOALAS, AND OTHER ANIMALS WITH
    POUCHES
OWLS, EAGLES, AND OTHER HUNTERS OF THE SKY
POISONOUS SNAKES
CATERPILLARS
SEALS, SEA LIONS, AND WALRUSES
ANIMALS WITH HORNS
ANIMALS THAT EAT OTHER ANIMALS
DUCKS, GEESE, AND SWANS

Each of the nature books in this series is planned to develop the child's powers of observation—to train him or her to notice distinguishing characteristics. A leaf is a leaf. A bird is a bird. An insect is an insect. That is true. But what makes an oak leaf different from a maple leaf? Why is a hawk different from an eagle, or a beetle different from a bug?

Classification is a painstaking science. These books give a child the essence of the search for differences that is the basis for scientific classification.

For the new Newman—Nicholas Robert

The authors wish to thank Patricia Escolante, Department of Ornithology, American Museum of Natural History, for reading the text of this book and offering many helpful suggestions.

Ducks, geese, and swans are waterbirds.
They dive, wade, and glide on lakes,
ponds, rivers, and seas all over the
world.

The three front toes of ducks,
geese, and swans are webbed.
This helps them swim.

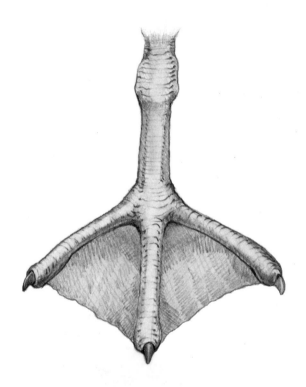

There is an old saying: "like water off a duck's back." Water rolls off the feathers of all waterbirds because the feathers are waxy. The wax keeps the water out and helps the bird stay dry and warm.

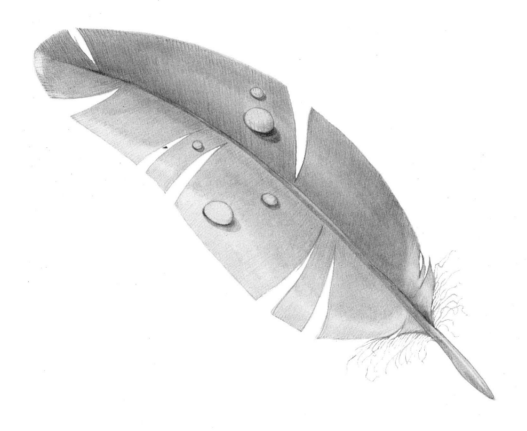

Ducks, geese, and swans come in all sizes
and shapes.

Some are big.
Some are small.
Some have long necks.
Some have short necks.
Some have wide, flat bills.
Some have thin, pointy bills.

10

How do we tell them apart?

Swans are the biggest.
They have the longest necks
and the heaviest bodies.

12

Most geese are not as big as swans
or as small as ducks.
They are middle-sized.

Ducks are the smallest.
They have short necks and short legs.
Their bills are flat and wide.
Most male and female ducks do not look alike.

Male

Female

Here are two white swans.
You can tell them apart by the way
they hold their necks when they are swimming.

Find the swan that holds its neck straight up.

Find the one that holds its neck like
the letter S.

Mute Swan

14

Whistling Swan

15

Match these swans to their names:

Black Swan
Black-necked Swan

GEESE

Every fall flocks of noisy
geese fly south,
honking all the way.
They fly in line or V formation.

Canada Geese can be told by their white
"chinstraps."

These two geese can also be told by their markings.

Which goose has black strips on its white head?
Which one is white with black wingtips?

Bar-headed Goose

Snow Goose

These two geese look almost alike.
But the Barnacle Goose has a white face
and the Brant Goose does not.

Which is which?

The Pygmy Goose is the smallest goose.
It can weigh less than an apple.

DUCKS

Some ducks feed just below the water.
Only their tails can be seen sticking
up in the air.
They are called Dabbling Ducks.

Dabbling Ducks take off by flying
straight up in the air.

The markings can help you tell Dabbling
Ducks apart.
Look for the duck with a white ring
around its neck.
Look for the one with white stripes,
patches, and spots.

Wood Duck

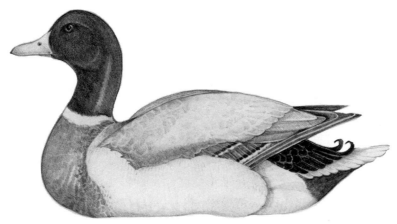

Mallard Duck

Sometimes the tail can be a clue.
This duck has a long needle-shaped tail.

Pintail Duck

Sometimes the bill can be a clue.
This duck has a spoon-shaped bill.

Shoveller Duck

25

Diving Ducks swim under the water to feed.

They run across the water to take off.

Here are two diving ducks.
The Black Scoter (*skoh*-ter) has a knob on its bill.

The Eider (*eye*-der) looks as if it is
wearing eyeglasses.

Which is which?

MERGANSERS

Mergansers are diving ducks that have
long, thin, bills with
saw-toothed edges.
The small fish they
feed on get caught in the edges.

Many mergansers have crests.

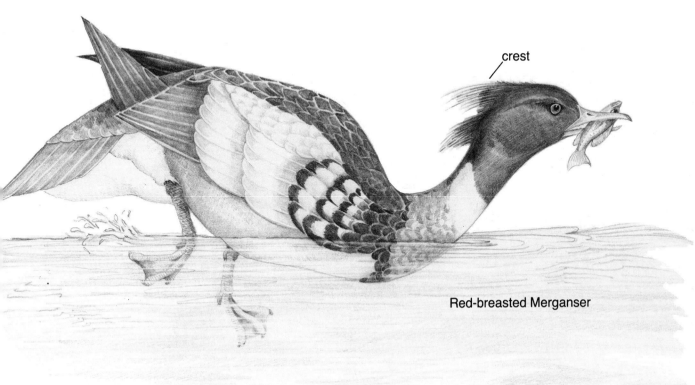

crest

Red-breasted Merganser

29

To tell ducks, geese, and swans apart:

Look at the size.

Look at the way they hold their necks.

Look at the bills.

Look at the markings.

Look at the tails.

Look for crests.

Look at the way they take off.

DUCKS, GEESE AND SWANS IN THIS BOOK

Bar-headed Goose   18
Barnacle Goose   20
Black Scoter Duck   27
Black Swan   16
Black-necked Swan   16
Brant Goose   20
Canada Goose   17
Eider Duck   27
Mallard Duck   24
Mute Swan   14
Pintail Duck   25
Pygmy Goose   21
Red-Breasted Merganser Duck   29
Shoveller Duck   25
Snow Goose   19
Whistling Swan   15
Wood Duck   24